FIRENZE
MVSEI

Pitti Palace
Palatine Gallery
and
Royal Apartments

MARCO CHIARINI
Director of the Palatine Gallery

D0964017

s i l l a b e

ISBN 88-86392-55-9
© 1998 s i l l a b e s.r.l.
Scali d'Azeglio, 22/24 - 57123 Livorno
tel. fax 0586.829931 - 0586.208826

managing editor: *Maddalena Paola Winspeare*
graphic design and cover: *Laura Belforte*
editing: *Federica Lehmann*
translation: *Heather Mackay Roberts*
translation of the introduction: *Harriet Paterson, Marina Pugliano*

series design: *Franco Bulletti*
photolithography: *La Nuova Lito-Firenze*

reproduction rights:
Archivio sillabe (foto P. Nannoni - S. Garbari)
Archivio Fotografico SBAS Firenze

CONTENTS

Enough books have been written about the public museums in Florence run by the Fine Arts and Historic Works Commission to fill a large library. This is hardly surprising when one considers that the artistic heritage preserved in our museums has been famous throughout the world for centuries. For hundreds of years writer and scholars, travellers of every nationality and country have been attempting to describe all that the Florentine museums contain. They have made great efforts to explain why these museums are so fascinating, and to lead a path through paintings and sculptures for both the uninformed but willing visitor and the refined and jaded intellectual.

Over time, however, the museums have altered their aspect and their layout, the exhibitions have been arranged in new ways, the collections have been enriched (or impoverished). Attributions of works in the museums have also changed, restorations have transformed the appearance of many pieces, the rise and fall of aesthetic tendencies have led to reorganisation and the exhibition of differing works. All these things are constantly taking place within the public collections because museology and the history of art, like any intellectual endeavour, are in a constant state of progress and transformation. This explains why the literature surrounding the Florentine museums (like that of any of the world's great art collections) is so immense, and in a process of continual updating and change.

The perfect, definitive guide to a museum, any museum, does not and cannot exist.

The premise seems obvious, but is nonetheless necessary in order to understand the point of the publication introduced by these lines. From the moment when, in accordance with the application of the Ronchey law 4/93, the Giunti publishing house group took over the running of the support services within the Florentine museum system, it was decided to start at once on a standardised series of illustrated guides. These guides, displaying the cuneiform flower of "Firenze Musei" on the cover, guarantee that at the year of publication the state of each museum is exactly that described in the guide.

Certain things are obviously necessary if a museum guide is to aspire to reliability, official standing and at the same time enjoy a wide distribution: accuracy of information, high quality reproductions, an easily manageable format, a reasonable cost and – not least – a clearly written text (without, naturally, being banal or lacking in precision). Readers will judge for themselves if the guide which follows this introduction reaches these standards. I have no doubt that this will be a serious and committed judgement, just as myself and the Publisher of this guide have been serious and committed in attempting to meet the cultural needs of whoever visits our museums in the best way and with every possible care.

Antonio Paolucci
*Head of the Fine Arts
and Historic Works Commission
of Florence, Pistoia and Prato*

Pitti Palace
The birth of a museum

The massive Pitti Palace on Florence's left bank, the Oltrarno, was built for the Florentine banker Luca Pitti and is supposedly based on a design by Filippo Brunelleschi. It took some four hundred years to acquire its present appearance, various alterations and additions having been made to the original corpus, which was built on two storeys with seven windows overlooking the piazza. It now houses three superb collections, in the Palatine Gallery, the Museo degli Argenti and the Museum of Modern Art, but its long history as the palace of the ruling dynasties of Florence began with its acquisition by Cosimo I, later Grand Duke of Tuscany, in the middle of the sixteenth century. He commissioned Bartolomeo Ammanati (1558-70) to construct two wings at the back of the building, so forming the magnificent courtyard leading on to the slopes of Boboli. It was during this period that this land behind the palace was gradually transformed into the gardens bearing the same name. In the following decades further additions were made to the original block until, by the beginning of this century, the façade measured some 200 metres.

For three hundred years, from the second half of the sixteenth century until 1859, when the Grand Duchy of Tuscany was annexed to the unified Kingdom of Italy, the palace and its courtyard were the focus for dazzling public and dynastic events and celebrations. They were the scene of weddings, baptisms, and the funerals of the Medici and Hapsburg-Lorraines, who succeeded as rulers of Tuscany in 1736.

It was in this palace that the Medici accumulated the collections which make the Palatine Gallery so distinctive: Cardinal Leopoldo de' Medici enriching it mostly with Venetian paintings while the Grand Prince Ferdinand, the son of the Grand Duke Cosimo III de' Medici, contributed his exceptional Renaissance and Baroque collection. It was under the Hapsburg-Lorraines that the collections were arranged on the first floor of the palace, the Baroque "quadreria" or display preserved to the present day; they also added rooms and paintings in accordance with Neo-Classical taste. Officially opened to the public in 1828, under the House of Savoy the Palace came under state control, and was further amplified with the Volterrano wing, doubling the number of works on display.

One of the Gallery's most distinctive features is the arrangement of the paintings, densely packed to form a pleasing display of size and colour in harmony with the decoration of the ceilings, furniture and sculpture. Each room has a particular character and each takes its name from the scene frescoed on the ceiling; decoration begun under the Medici and continued by the Lorraines until well into the nineteenth century. The Lorraines were largely responsible for supplying the rooms with the furniture produced by the Opificio della Pietre Dure, the famous manufacture of Florentine mosaic work in precious and semi-precious stones, and with the precious objects which lend the rooms the particular opulence of both the Baroque and Neo-Classical periods.

Palatine Gallery

A monumental stairway in the right-hand corner of the courtyard leads to the entrance of the Palatine Gallery. It was called "Palatina", signifying that the gallery was "of the palace" of the ruling family, when first opened to the public by Leopold II of Lorraine in 1828. The Gallery occupies the most important rooms on the *piano nobile*, or first floor: six rooms overlooking the piazza and those in the north wing at the rear of the building, previously the winter apartments of the Medici Grand Dukes. When the ruling family vacated these rooms for those on the floor above they were used, from the end of the eighteenth century, for the permanent display of the finest paintings in the Pitti Palace, originally some five hundred works, collected for the most part by the Medici. It is difficult to imagine a more ideal setting than these rooms on the façade, magnificently decorated with frescoes and stucco by Pietro da Cortona and Ciro Ferri between 1641 and 1647. These housed the nucleus of the collection, notable for the number of large altarpieces and monumental works, and a tour of the collection would originally have begun in the first room, the Venus Room. For practical reasons vistors now enter from the Statue Gallery, with antique sculpture taken from the Villa Medici in Rome, and from the Castagnoli Room, in which stands the Table of the Muses, a supreme technical achievement produced by the Opificio delle Pietre Dure in 1853, and mounted on a bronze base by Giovanni Dupré.

The Castagnoli Room leads, on the right, into the Volterrano wing (sometimes closed). These were the private apartments of the Grand Duchesses from the time of Cosimo II de' Medici until the death here of the last of the family, Anna Maria Luisa, in 1743. At her death she bequeathed all the treasures of the Medici collections to the people of Florence to the perpetual enrichment of her city.

The sequence of the rooms was altered following their restoration and redecoration, begun in 1815.

ALLEGORIES ROOM (SALA DELLE ALLEGORIE)

Ceiling decorated with fresco and stucco work by Volterrano, for the Grand Duchess Vittoria della Rovere, the wife of Ferdinando II, in the middle of the seventeenth century.

VOLTERRANO
The Joke played on the Priest Arlotto
c. 1640
Tempera on canvas,
107 × 150 cm

Volterrano was the most Baroque of all the Florentine decorative painters in the seventeenth century. There are nevertheless traces of his early training with the late-Mannerist painter Giovanni da San Giovanni in his early works, also evident in this lively episode. It is one of many illustrating scenes from the life of Arlotto Mainardi, the parish priest of S. Cresci a Maciuoli, who was famous for his pranks. Here Volteranno, treating the figures with expressive energy, gives us a spirited interpretation of a party in the courtyard of a villa outside Florence.

11

EMILIO ZOCCHI
*Michelangelo
as a child*
1861
Marble, height 60 cm

This romantic depiction of Michelangelo as a child sculpting the head of a faun in the San Marco gardens, reflects popular local mytholo-gy surrounding the life of the great Florentine artist, recorded in the *Lives of the Artists* by Vasari.

Room of the Fine Arts (Sala delle Belle Arti)

Fresco depicting Jupiter sending Minerva to enkindle an interest in the Arts on earth *by Domenico Podestà (1817).*

CIGOLI

*The Martyrdom of
St Stephen*

1597
Oil on canvas, 480 × 287 cm

This altarpiece, painted in 1597 for the convent of Montedomini in Florence, became part of the Florentine galleries collection at the begin-ning of the nineteenth century and has been in the Pitti since 1928. Cigoli, then the leading painter of the Floren-tine school, shows re-markable success in creating an alternative to the dominant late Mannerist style in Italy. While Caravaggio re-volutionised painting with his unprecedented realism, Cigoli turned to Venetian painting, notably Tintoretto, to instil his works with a pictorial vitality usual-ly associated with Ba-roque painters, earning this painting the partic-ualr admiration of both Rubens and Pietro da Cortona.

HERCULES ROOM (SALA D'ERCOLE)

Decorated by Pietro Benvenuti in 1828 with the Labours of Hercules. *In the centre of the room stands a large Sèvres porcelain and gilt-bronze vase by Pierre Philippe Thomire.*

DAWN ROOM (SALA DELL'AURORA)

Gaspare Martelli painted the fresco of Dawn between 1815-17.

BERENICE ROOM (SALA DI BERENICE)

Frescoed by Giuseppe Bezzuoli with Titus abandoning Berenice *and figures of the* Cardinal Virtues *in the lunettes.*

PSYCHE ROOM (SALA DI PSICHE)

Frescoed by Giuseppe Collignon this room brings together the greatest collection of paintings by the Neapolitan, Salvator Rosa, dating from his Florentine period.

SALVATOR ROSA
Battle
c. 1640
Oil on canvas, 234 × 350 cm

This painting for Ferdinando II, Grand Duke of Tuscany, by the lively and genial Neapolitan Salvator Rosa, was executed at the beginning of his sojourn in Florence which lasted some ten years (c. 1640-49). He painted almost exclusively for the Medici and his additional involvement in literary and theatrical activities secured him a preminent position in Florentine culture of the period. His paintings in the Palatine Gallery started a vogue in European painting for battle scenes and this canvas is a superb example of the genre.

MUSIC ROOM (SALA DELLA MUSICA)

The private musical gatherings held in this room have influenced the style of the furniture and the decorative appliques. *The Neo-Classical room has columns in Sienese yellow and frescoes on the ceiling painted by Luigi Ademollo (c. 1815) illustrating episodes from the Seige of Vienna of 1683 when the Imperial army defeated the Turk together with a remarkable monochrome trompe l'oeil frieze imitating sculpture in low-relief. The gilt-bronze and malachite table was made by Pierre Philippe Thomire in 1819.*

POCCETTI CORRIDOR (CORRIDOIO DEL POCCETTI)

The frescoes on the ceiling by Matteo Rosselli and assistants, were once attributed to Bernardo Barbatelli, known as Poccetti.

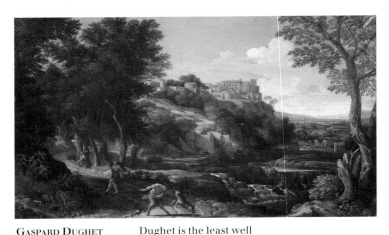

GASPARD DUGHET
*Landscape with
a dancing faun*
c. 1667-68
Oil on canvas, 51 × 87 cm

Dughet is the least well known of the three French painters who revolutionised landscape painting in the seventeenth and eighteenth centuries. Brother-in-law to Nicholas Poussin, he was initially influenced by Poussin's classical treatment of landscape but later became susceptible to Claude Lorraine's greater naturalism. The painting is one of four.

FRANCESCO FURINI

Hylas and the Nymphs

c. 1655
Oil on canvas, 230 × 261 cm

Francesco Furini gained considerable renown both for his revival of the *sfumato* technique, or shading, introduced by Leonardo, no longer used in the seventeenth century, and for his ability to render the female body in all its seductive charm. This painting, his masterpiece, was painted for Agnolo Galli and purchased for the Florentine galleries at the beginning of this century. Furini has invented a pictorial dream in which the intertwining nymphs create an impression of overwhelming sensuality.

Prometheus Room (Sala di Prometeo)

The fine fresco decoration by Giuseppe Collignon (c. 1830-40) shows the Chariot of the Sun *and* Prometheus bringing fire to man. *The room houses the oldest paintings in the collections including fifteenth-century Florentine tondos.*

The fine vase decorated with brightly coloured bunches of flowers and gilt-bronze mounts was produced by the Sevres factory in 1844 after a design by L. Schilt.

PONTORMO

Adoration of the Magi

1520
Oil on canvas, 85 × 191 cm

Recent restoration has revealed the painting's dazzling colours and superb draughtsmanship (see the detail above), reflecting the influence of Northern painting, on the twenty-seven year old Pontormo, the same influence apparent in his frescoes in the Certosa monastery at Galluzzo. In this detailed composition a debt to Michelangelo is also discernible combined with a narrative strain well suited to the private nature of the commission. Together with other panels by Granacci, Franciabigio and Andrea del Sarto it was intended to decorate a room in the palazzo of Giovanni Maria Benintendi. The figure looking out of the painting is a self-portrait of Pontormo.

BOTTICELLI

Portrait of a young man wearing a "mazzocchio"

c. 1470
Oil on panel, 51 × 54 cm

This small and little known portrait of a young man wearing the typical Florentine headdress of the period is a fine example of a genre which first appeared in Florence in the early fifteenth century and was developed in a distinctive way by Botticelli. Clearly derived from the work of Paolo Uccello and Andrea del Castagno, the portrait with its slightly turned, three-quarter pose is here given an unprecedented individuality. The surface of the painting has suffered from over enthusiastic cleaning in the past.

FILIPPO LIPPI

*Virgin and Child
with Scenes from
the Life of St Anne
("Tondo Bartolini")*

c. 1450
Oil on panel, diam. 135 cm

Little is known either of the patron or of the intended destination of this large tondo "da stanza" of the early fifteenth century, first mentioned in the Pitti in the seventeenth century. There is a large autograph drawing on the back of the painting of a coat of arms very like that of the Martelli family for whom Lippi worked so the painting may well have been a Martelli commission. In this tondo, the only one produced by Lippi and one of the largest painted in the Quattrocento, he still relies on the medieval tradition of bringing together various episodes in a single painting. The Virgin is enthroned with the Christ Child on her knee, holding up a seed from an opened pomegranite, a symbol of His Passion and

Death. Behind the Virgin to the right, her parents Anne and Joachim meet at the Golden Gate; to the left St Anne gives birth to Mary while in the middle distance on the right female figures are shown bearing gifts to St Anne. The composition is unified by the skilful use of perspective, creating well-defined chromatic areas which also serve as an effective foil to the figures in movement. The linear elegance of the painting is a prelude to the achievements of Filippo Lippi's most celebrated pupil, Sandro Botticelli.

CORRIDOR OF THE COLUMNS (CORRIDOIO DELLE COLONNE)

This corridor takes its name from two alabaster columns standing at one end and has walls covered with a series of small Dutch and Flemish paintings.

Justice Room (Sala della Giustizia)

Fresco by Antonio Fedi (after 1815).

Titian
Portrait of Tommaso Mosti (?)
c. 1520-30
Oil on canvas, 85 × 66 cm

This fine portrait was bought for the collection of Cardinal Leopoldo de' Medici as a portrait of Tommaso Mosti, a courtier in Urbino. It was only after restoration this century that it was unanimously accepted as the work of Titian, and recognised as a masterpiece of the early years of his maturity. The degree of psychological penetration in the depiction of the young man's face and the incomparable skill in the rendering of the fur-lined jacket and the other details of his costume in tones of black grey and white are typical of Titian's best work.

FLORA ROOM (SALA DI FLORA)

Ceiling fresco of an allegory of Flora painted by Antonio Marini (after 1815).

ALESSANDRO ALLORI
Madonna and Child
c. 1590
Oil on canvas, 133 × 94 cm

This delightful picture, painted after the Council of Trent, clearly reflects the spirit of court art in its elegance and formal perfection. Alessandro Allori trained in the workshop of his uncle, Bronzino, to whom he was strongly indebted, reinterpreting his models in the sweeter style prevalent in the courts of Europe at the end of the sixteenth century.

ANTONIE VAN DYCK

Rest During the Flight into Egypt

c. 1630

Oil on canvas, 131 × 195 cm

This painting was acquired for the Palatine Gallery, along with others, from the Gerini Gallery in 1818.

Generally considered to be a workshop piece from the artist's English period, and a minor version of an analogous composition now found in the Hermitage Museum in St Petersburg. A recent restoration has dispelled former doubts concerning the identity of the painter, since the painting has been shown to be almost completely by the great Flemish artist (the small angels in the top right corner perhaps made the identification easier). Famous as a portraitist, Van Dyck – who was Peter Paul Rubens' most brilliant student – also dealt with religious and mythological themes, although more rarely. In this painting, the pictorial and chromatic delicacy that the artist achieved after his move to England, where he was a painter in the court of Charles I, is clearly evident.

PERUGINO

Mary Magdalen

c. 1496-1500
Oil on panel, 47 × 34 cm

The gold letters on her
bodice read: S. MARIA
MADALENA.

This work epitomises
the alluring serenity
which made Perugino,
and hence the Umbri-
an school, so popular.
Here he combines the
use of *chiaroscuro* or
shading, in the manner
of Leonardo, with the
attention to minute de-
tail of the Flemish
school in a distinctly
personal synthesis.

ROOM OF THE CUPIDS (SALA DEI PUTTI)

Ceiling decoration by Antonio Marini (c. 1830).

RACHEL RUYSCH
Still-life
1716
Oil on canvas, 89 × 79 cm

This work, dated 1716 was painted as the *pendant*, or companion piece, to an exuberant *Vase of flowers* and was acquired by Ferdinand III of Lorraine for the Gallery in the Pitti Palace at the beginning of the nineteenth century. Ruysch, the daughter of a botanist and the pupil of Willem van Aelst, here displays her unrivalled technical virtuosity as one of the last exponents of this genre which flourished in Holland in the seventeenth century.

WILLEM VAN AELST
Still-life
1652
Oil on canvas, 77 × 102 cm

Van Aelst enjoyed great popularity in Rome and more especially in Florence where he was for a long time employed by the Medici, creating many works still in the Florentine collections. He was trained in the great tradition of Dutch seventeenth century still-life painting, combining sumptuous colour and detail with acute realism, as in this still-life depicting precious pieces from the Medici collections, still in the Pitti (Museo degli Argenti). A *Still-life with fruit* painted as a *pendant* is also in the Gallery.

PETER PAUL RUBENS
The Three Graces
c. 1620-23
Oil on canvas, 47 × 34 cm

Cardinal Leopoldo de' Medici was a great ad-mirer of Flemish paint-ing and he added this *grisaille* to his collection which also included a large number of sketch-es. This small painting was designed as the subject for an ivory vase, a decorative tech-nique extremely popu-lar in Northern Europe in the sixteenth and sev-enteenth centuries.

ULYSSES ROOM (SALA DI ULISSE)

Gaspare Martelli frescoed the ceiling with the Return of Ulysses, *alluding to the return to Florence of the Grand Duke Ferdinand III of Lorraine in 1815.*

FILIPPINO LIPPI
The death of Lucretia
c. 1470
Oil on panel, 42 × 126 cm

This painting is the length of a wedding chest, a typical piece of Florentine furniture in the Quattrocento. A companion work depicting the *Death of the Virgin* is in the Louvre. Filippino, the son of Fra' Filippo Lippi, trained with Sandro Botticelli and his work aspires to the same linear beauty which here animates the various episodes to create a lively narrative against the architectural unity of the background.

RAPHAEL

*Madonna and
Child, St John the
Baptist and Saints
("Madonna
dell'impannata")*

c. 1514
Oil on canvas, 160 × 127 cm

This Virgin and Child
commissioned for Bin-
di Altoviti, a banker for
the Papal curia, has an
interesting history. X-
ray treatment has re-
vealed St Joseph hold-
ing the Baptist in his
arms underneath the
existing figure of the in-
fant John, now looking
straight out of the pic-
ture. The composition
was simplified in order
to keep the group en-
closed around the cen-
tral figure of the Christ
Child. The painting,
called the Madonna of
the "impannata" be-
cause of the cloth cov-
ering the window in the
background to the
right, was added to the
Medici collections at
the time of Cosimo I.

ANDREA DEL SARTO
Madonna and Child with Saints ("Pala di Gambassi")
1525-26
Oil on canvas, 215 × 175 cm

This altarpiece, commissioned by a friend of the painter, "Becuccio bicchieraio", or Becuc-cio the glass-maker, from Gambassi c. 1525-26, echoes motifs already used by del Sarto *(Trinity*, Saturn Room) in an extraordinarily graceful composition, enhanced by the soft tones and sophisticated colouring. Portraits of Becuccio and his wife were painted in two tondi (now in the Art Institute of Chicago) and inserted in a predella panel which has since been lost.

Cigoli

Ecce Homo

c. 1604-6

Oil on canvas, 175 × 135 cm

Cigoli's most famous work was painted at the same time as an *Ecce Homo* by Caravaggio, and was judged superior. Cigoli gives the theme a highly dramatic but intensely religious interpretation and the composition is emblematic of religious art in the counter-reformation. The passages of thicker brushwork and the references to Venetian painting were imitated, not least by Cigoli most successful pupils, Domenico Fetti and Cristofano Allori.

NAPOLEON'S BATHROOM (BAGNO DI NAPOLEONE)

This Neo-Classical bathroom built for Napoleon Bonaparte by his sister, Elisa Baciocchi, Grand Duchess of Tuscany, between 1808 and 1813 was designed by Giuseppe Cacialli.

EDUCATION OF JUPITER ROOM
(SALA DELL'EDUCAZIONE DI GIOVE)

Frescoes by Luigi Catani commissioned as decoration for the bedroom intended for Napoleon Bonaparte (c. 1811-15).

CARLO DOLCI
St Andrew before the Cross
1646
Oil on canvas, 122 × 99 cm

This version of the subject, and there are several others, was painted for Carlo Gerini. In 1818 it was acquired for the Palatine Gallery together with other pictures from the same collection. Despite the large number of paintings in the gallery by Dolci, who enjoyed the patronage of the Grand Duchess Vittoria della Rovere (her portrait by Dolci is in the Saturn Room) this highly accomplished work was a significant addition to the Gallery.

CARAVAGGIO
Sleeping Cupid
1608
Oil on canvas, 71 × 105 cm

Caravaggio, born near Milan, introduced a startling new realism into European painting. This *Sleeping Cupid* was produced in 1608 during his stay in Malta for a member of the Order of Malta, the Florentine Niccolò dell'Antella. Recent research has shown that Caravaggio's model was a dead child as the body bears signs of a fatal infantile infection. By supplying the sleeping corpse with wings and an arrow Caravaggio deconsecrated the traditional interpretation of sweet and ethereal Love to create a powerful, dramatic and contemporary image.

CRISTOFANO ALLORI
Judith holding the head of Holofernes
c. 1620
Oil on canvas, 139 × 116 cm

This painting by Cristofano Allori, allegedly the son of the late Mannerist follower of Bronzino, Alessandro Allori, although unfinished (Judith's cloak, for example, has no clasp or cord) is a masterpiece of the new realism of the early decades of the seventeenth century. Allori, in his treatment of the subject was strongly influenced by the intense realism of Caravaggio, and was also conscious of the interpretation by Artemisia Gentileschi (*Judith*, Iliad Room). Holofernes's head is a self-portrait of the artist while his mistress Mazzafirra is depicted as Judith holding his head by the hair. This picture made a powerful impact when first created and was understandably much admired by Romantic painters.

STOVE ROOM (SALA DELLA STUFA)

The adjacent room, the Stove Room, which once housed the heating pipes to warm the neighbouring bedrooms, was decorated, between 1638 and 1641, for Ferdinando III by Pietro da Cortona with a cycle showing the Four Ages of Man.

ILIAD ROOM (SALA DELL'ILIADE)

Frescoes on the ceiling depict scenes from Mount Olympus while the lunettes are decorated with episodes from Homer's Iliad *(1819-25), painted by Luigi Sabatelli.*

ARTEMISIA GENTILESCHI
Judith
c. 1614-20
Oil on canvas, 117×93 cm

A powerful and dramatic picture with the mirror positioning of the two turned, or *contrapposto*, figures and a chromatic range derived from Caravaggio and from the painter's father, Orazio. This work, together with the *Magdalen*, also painted during Artemisia Gentileschi's stay at the court of Tuscany from 1613-20, had a profound influence on Florentine painting at the time (see Cristofano Allori, *Judith*, Education of Jupiter Room).

JUSTUS SUSTERMANS

*Portrait of Prince
Mattias de' Medici*
c. 1660
Oil on canvas, 76 × 60 cm

Sustermans, who ar-
rived at the Florentine
court in 1619-20, then
served as the official
painter of the Medici
until his death some six-
ty years later. His spir-
ited style developed af-
ter his early training
with Pourbus, whose
influence is apparent in
another portrait by
Sustermans of *Walde-
mar Christian, Prince of
Denmark*, also in this
room. He was a friend
of Rubens and was in-
fluenced by both Van
Dyck and Velazquez.
Sustermans's absorp-
tion of the Baroque
conception of painting
are fully evident in the
chromatic range and
internal dynamics in
this lively depiction of
Prince Mattias de'
Medici, governor of
Siena.

ANDREA DEL SARTO
Assumption of the Virgin ("Assunta Panciatichi")

1522-23
Oil on panel, 362 × 209 cm

This enormous altarpiece, commissioned by Bartolomeo Panciatichi for the altar of his chapel in the church of Notre-Dame du Confort in Lyons, never reached its destination but was purchased for the Medici collections in the middle of the seventeenth century.

The monumental and revolutionary composition with the dramatic division of the episode on two levels and Andrea del Sarto's use of shot and strongly contrasting colours had a lasting impact on sixteenth and seventeenth century painting and gained this picture admiration from Rubens. Andrea del Sarto adopted the same composition in 1526 in his altarpiece of the same subject for the Passerini family in Cortona, also acquired by the Medici at the end of the seventeenth century. The altarpiece is still positioned opposite the earlier painting according to the dictates of nineteenth-century taste which favoured the aesthetics of display based on a harmony of shape, size and colour.

RAPHAEL
*Portrait of a woman
("La Gravida")*
c. 1507
Oil on panel, 66 × 52 cm

This dignified portrait of a pregnant woman is one of the finest portraits painted by the young Raphael during his last stay in Florence. The bold colouring of the woman's garment against the dense, dark background and the painting's formal complexity distinguish this work from those executed during Raphael's first Roman period.

RIDOLFO DEL GHIRLANDAIO
*Portrait of a
Woman*
1508
Oil on panel, 61 × 47 cm

This portrait, the work of the gifted son of the more famous Domenico Ghirlandaio, is clearly indebted to Raphael's portrait painting of his Florentine period.

ANNIBALE CARRACCI
Christ in glory with Saints
c. 1597-98
Oil on canvas, 194 × 142 cm

Annibale Carracci is the Bolognese painter whose work clearly marks the transition from the late sixteenth to the new century and the beginnings of the Baroque style. He united the Tuscan-Roman approach to drawing with Venetian colouring to create a novel synthesis reflected in this composition painted for Cardinal Odoardo Farnese, portrayed in the lower left of the painting. The painting was acquired by Ferdinando de' Medici at the end of the seventeenth century.

VERONESE
The Baptism of Christ
c. 1575
Oil on canvas, 196 × 133 cm

A work from Veronese's mature period it is stylistically reminiscent of the *Preaching of the Baptist* (Rome, Villa Borghese) while the colours suffused in a warm, golden light are typical of Veronese's late works.

SATURN ROOM (SALA DI SATURNO)

Frescoes and stucco by Ciro Ferri, the pupil of Pietro da Cortona, who here worked following the designs of his master between 1663-65. Here the prince, in the guise of Hercules, ascends Mount Olympus to be greeted by the gods while the four lunettes depict scenes from the lives of Scipio, Lycurgus, Sylla and Syrus.

RAPHAEL

Madonna and Child ("Madonna del Granduca")

c. 1506
Oil on panel, 84.5 × 55.9 cm

This Virgin and Child is known as the " Madonna del Granduca" because it was acquired by the Grand Duke Ferdinand III of Lorraine when in exile during the Napoleon period in Tuscany. It is one of several "Belle Madonne" painted during Raphael's visits to Florence before 1507, but this is not only the simplest but also the most moving portrayal of the Holy Mother and Child. Inspired by Leonardo's use of *chiaroscuro* in the soft modelling of the figures emerging from the dark ground, Raphael also reveals his precise drawing and "geometrical" conception of form, acquired in the workshop of Perugino. The painting is unusual in comparison with other treatments of the same theme in that a landscape background is here eliminated in favour of a dense, dark ground, focusing attention fully on the Madonna and Child.

ANDREA DEL SARTO
Dispute on the Trinity
1517
Oil on panel, 232 × 193 cm

This solemn assembly of saints with St Augustine, St Lawrence, St Dominic and St Francis standing and the Magdalen and St John the Baptist kneeling in the foreground, echoes Raphael's magnificent fresco in the Vatican and must have created a powerful impact when placed above the altar in the Augustinian church of San Gallo. Painted in 1517, the quality of the work lies in the beauty of the colouring combined with soft shading derived from Leonardo together with the strength of Michelangelo's modelling of form.

RAPHAEL

Portrait of Tommaso Inghirami ("Fedra")
c. 1510
Oil on panel 89.5 × 62.3 cm

Inghirami, a nobleman from Volterra and friend of Leo X de' Medici, who created him librarian at the Vatican, is here depicted in the more powerful of the two portraits attributed to Raphael (the other is in the Isabella Stewart Gardner Collection, Boston). Raphael's portrait of Tommaso Inghirami (nick-named Fedra in allusion to his part in the play by Seneca) probably dates to 1510, the year he was nominated cardinal. The portrait reflects a new monumentality in the treatment of the half figure, with his head turned to conceal a squint, and marks the beginning of Raphael's Roman period.

RAPHAEL
*Portrait of
Agnolo Doni*
1505-06
Oil on panel, 65 × 45.7 cm

RAPHAEL
*Portrait of
Maddalena Doni*
c. 1505-06
Oil on panel, 65 × 45.7 cm

This fine portrait was painted as the companion to one of Agnolo's wife, Maddalena Strozzi, perhaps forming a diptych in the style of Piero della Francesca's portrayal of the Duke and Duchess of Urbino. The couple were married in 1503 but the portrait of Agnolo is later than that of Maddalena as the landscape background does not conceal an interior view, initially applied to his wife's portrait. The Doni were great art collectors (Donatello) and commissioned the *Holy* *Family* from Michelangelo which still bears their name (*Tondo Doni*, Uffizi).

The portrait is clearly influenced by Leonardo's painting of the *Mona Lisa* (Louvre). X-ray research has revealed that Raphael originally draughted the figure seated in a room, later substituted for the enchanting spring landscape which serves as the transculent link uniting the two Doni portraits. Both paintings reveal a close attention to minute detail, especially of dress and jewellery, so characteristic of Flemish painting (Memling).

RAPHAEL
The Vision of Ezechiel
c. 1518
Oil on panel, 47.7 × 29.5 cm

This small painting, painted in 1518 for a member of the Her-colani family, was later bought by Francesco I de' Medici. It concentrates all the formal strength evident in Raphael's work during his last years in Rome, culminating in the Vatican *Transfiguration*.

Both works reflect the same concentration of energy and the sublime imagination which Raphael deployed in the creation of a naturalistic cosmic vision based on a complex balance of form, light and colour.

RAPHAEL
Madonna del Baldacchino
c. 1508
Oil on panel, 279 × 217 cm

This painting was unfinished when Raphael left Florence for the last time to work at the Papal court in Rome. It was commissioned by Benedetto Dei for the altar of the family chapel in the church of Santo Spirito, but was never put in place. A large altarpiece by Rosso Fiorentino, now also in the Pitti in the Apollo Room, was hung there instead. Although the painting is unfinished, most noticeably in the two angels in the foreground, the composition shows an unprecedented architectural grandeur and complexity: the throne is set in a semicircular chapel with columns in imitation of those designed by Brunelleschi for Santo Spirito, breaking with the tradition of the fifteenth-century Florentine "Sacra Conversazione".

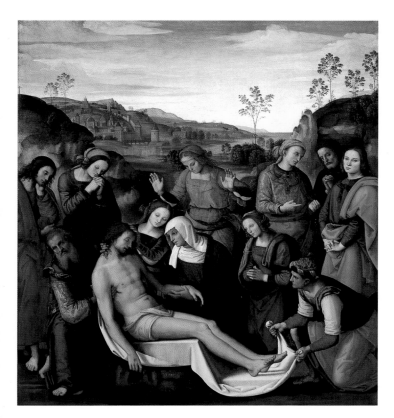

PERUGINO

Lamentation

1495
Oil on panel, 214 × 195 cm

Perugino, influenced at an early age by Piero della Francesca, introduced the Umbrian style to Florence when he continued his training in Verrocchio's workshop. Perugino's importance lies in the serene classicism of his pictures with large areas devoted to the depiction of landscape, a trait apparent in the work of his most gifted pupil, Raphael. This *Lamentation*, painted for the convent of the Poor Clares in Florence, is typical of the controlled lyricism of Perugino's composition set in a dreamy landscape, later echoed by Raphael in his panel of the *Entombment* painted for Atalanta Baglioni in 1507 (Rome, Villa Borghese).

Raphael

Madonna and Child with St John the Baptist ("Madonna della Seggiola")

c. 1516
Oil on panel, diam. 71 cm

The most famous of Raphael's Madonnas, it belongs to the artist's highly productive late period in Rome, and although it is uncertain who commissioned the work it may well have been Pope Leo X de' Medici. Raphael made a number of paintings of the Virgin and Child but this is the only tondo, reviving the circular composition popular in Florence, used once by Michelangelo in his painting of the *Tondo Doni* (Uffizi) and twice in his sculpture (*Tondo Taddei*, Royal Academy, London; *Tondo Pitti*, Bargello Museum, Florence). It was not these however that provided Raphael's inspiration but the more distant works of Donatello, showing Mother and Child in close embrace which had already attracted him during his Florentine period (*Madonna Tempi*, Alte Pinakothek, Munich). In this composition the intertwined forms create a more complex rhythm, more monumental and underscored by full, glowing, almost Venetian colouring.

Jupiter Room (Sala di Giove)

Once the throne room of the Grand Ducal apartments, it was decorated with stucco and frescoes by Pietro da Cortona, between 1642 and 1644.

ANDREA DEL SARTO
St John the Baptist
c. 1523
Oil on panel, 94 × 68 cm

Although commissioned as a private devotional painting the decisive bearing and forthright stance of the young John the Baptist suggest a public work and have gained it great popularity. The sculptural quality of the figure enhanced by the soft shading or *sfumato* derived from Leonardo, together with the classical pose in the manner of Raphael, are seen to full advantage swathed in the red mantle, foreshadowing the dramatic contrasts favoured by Caravaggio.

GIOVANNI LANFRANCO
The ecstasy of Saint Margherita of Cortona
1622
Oil on canvas, 230 × 185 cm

Painted in 1622 by the Emilian Lanfranco for the altar of the Venuti in Santa Maria Nuova in Cortona it was obtained directly from Cortona for the collection of Ferdinando de' Medici. Lanfranco was one of the earliest exponents of the Baroque manner, exemplified in this composition full of movement and suffused with transcendental light.

FRA' BARTOLOMEO

Pietà

c. 1511-12
Oil on panel,
158 × 199 cm

Despite the loss of the top section of this painting, originally an altarpiece for the church of San Gallo, it remains one of the most influential works of the early sixteenth century in Florence. It shows a powerful debt to Raphael's classicism which Fra' Bartolomeo combines with a purity and fluidity of design and an intense chromatic range, reminiscent of Venetian painting.

RAPHAEL

Portrait of a Young Woman ("La Velata")

c. 1516
Oil on canvas, 82 × 60.5 cm

With this portrait of an unknown, veiled woman (modern scholarship has exploded the romantic tale linking her of Raphael's mythical lover, "La Fornarina") the artist's creative journey comes to an entirely original and unmistakable conclusion, having passed through the Florentine experiences (Leonardo) whose influence is noticeable in other female portraits in the Pitti (*Maddalena Doni*, *La Gravida*). From the sculptural feeling of those pictures we come to a diffused luminosity and a freedom of technique that can only be explained as the result of Raphael's new pictorial mastery acquired while working on the frescoes in the Vatican *Stanze*. The loveliness of the face framed by the veil, recalling Antonello da Messina's *Virgin Annunciate*, is matched by the bravura "set piece" of the ruched silken sleeve, an inimitable pictorial *tour de force*. The intensity of the sitter's gaze and the beauty of her face (she is possibly the same model as that used for the *Sistine Madonna* now in Dresden) linger in the memory, as summits of formal perfection never to be reached again.

GIORGIONE
The Three Ages of Man
c. 1500
Oil on panel, 62 × 77 cm

The allegorical significance of this painting is now rejected and it is seen rather as a singing lesson or "concert of voices", typical of the musical Venetian culture to which Giorgione belonged. The attribution to Giorgione is fairly recent; other Venetian artists, including Bellini and Lotto having at various times been linked to the painting. The modern consensus is that this is a youthful work, strongly reminiscent of both Bellini and Leonardo, but already rich in motifs that the artist would develop in later years.

MARS ROOM (SALA DI MARTE)

On the ceiling an allegory of War and Peace surrounds a triumphal vision of the Medici coat of arms, painted by Pietro da Cortona between 1644 and 1646.

BARTOLOMÉ ESTEBAN MURILLO
Madonna and Child
c. 1650
Oil on canvas, 157 × 107 cm

The example of Raphael is very clearly present in this sweet *Madonna and Child*. Instead of the *chiaroscuro* contrasts typical of Murillo's more youthful productions, such as the *Madonna of the Rosary* in the same room, there is here soft modelling with transparent and almost pastel colours that pervade the figures with interior light. The picture may have been acquired by Ferdinando II de' Medici.

PETER PAUL RUBENS
The four philosophers
c. 1611-12
Oil on panel, 164 × 139 cm

Rubens painted this large quadruple portrait around 1611-12, in memory of his brother Philip, a pupil of the philosopher Justus Lipsius, who is also shown. Both men had recently died. The artist portrayed himself in upper left, and in the lower right he added Jan van de Wouvere, a fellow student of Philip's. The four tulips beside the bust of Seneca (which Rubens acquired in Rome) symbolise the lives of the four sitters (two have already opened out). The books lying on the carpet-covered table, the view of the Palatine hill in the background, the gestures and the intensity of the glances make this group portrait a masterpiece of seventeenth-century art.

PETER PAUL RUBENS
The consequences of war
1637-38
Oil on canvas,
206 × 345 cm

The allegorical title obscures the painting's true subject: on the left Europe, dressed in black, casts her eyes and her hands upwards before the open-doored temple of Janus, while in the centre naked Venus endeavours to restrain Mars, who grasps a shield and a drawn sword as he strides into battle, dragged by the Furies. In his march he tramples on books and overturns the Arts, as well as a young woman with a baby at her breast. Sending this painting in 1638 to his colleague Justus Sustermans, court painter to the Medici, Rubens explained its meaning in relation to the Thirty Years' War which was raging in his homeland. A late masterpiece of the great Flemish painter, the picture is also an open homage to Italian art of the full Renaissance, from Titian onwards.

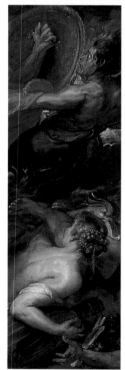

ANDREA DEL SARTO

Stories from the Life of Joseph

1515-16
Oil on panel, 98 × 135 cm

These two panels, painted in 1515-16 for the bridal chamber of Pierfrancesco Borgherini and Margherita Acciaioli (together with works by Pontormo, Granacci and Bachiacca, now dispersed in various museums in Europe) soon became so celebrated that they were sought by Francis I of France. It was however Francesco I de' Medici who acquired them in 1584 and exhibited them in the Tribuna of the Uffizi Gallery from where they were brought to the Pitti a century later. The Florentine painter arranges the complex narrative of the episodes from the life of Joseph into clearly defined groups, unified in their translucent vision of an Egyptian landscape dominated by Renaissance architectural splendours and dazzling fifteenth-century costumes.

VERONESE
*Portrait of a man
in furs*
c. 1550-60
Oil on canvas,
140 × 107 cm

TITIAN
*Portrait of Ippolito
de' Medici*
1533
Oil on canvas,
139 × 107 cm

Paolo Veronese, the third great Venetian painter of the full Renaissance, is especially famous for his sacred and mythological scenes which decorate the churches and palazzi of Venice and the Veneto. However he also, if rarely, attempted portraits, and managed to achieve a personal manner in a genre at which both Titian and Tintoretto excelled.
This is certainly true of the monumental portrait of a gentleman in the Pitti Gallery, which although influenced by Titian's portraits attains a highly individual style most evident in the superb painterly treatment of the furs.

Ippolito de' Medici, son of Giuliano Duke of Nemours, was created cardinal at the age of eighteen by Clement VII. More interested in war than a career in the Church, he had himself painted by Titian when he was in Bologna in 1533, dressed in the Hungarian style in memory of his role in the siege of Vienna by the Turks. The harmony of violet and magenta emphasise the martial bearing and somewhat cruel expression of the youthful warrior.

ANTHONY VAN DYCK
Portrait of Cardinal Bentivoglio
c. 1625
Oil on canvas,
195 × 147 cm

TINTORETTO
Portrait of Alvise Cornaro
c. 1560-65
Oil on canvas,
113 × 85 cm

This extraordinary symphony of red – the colour of the cardinalate – was meant to celebrate the elevation to the Sacred College of Guido Bentivoglio. His portrait is the concluding masterpiece of the Italian period of the greatest genius among Rubens's pupils. The full-length, life-sized figure dominates its surroundings with the nobility of its lineaments, the elegance of the hands, the refinement of the clothing. The cardinal emerges from the background with a majestic presence, subtly controlled by acute psychological insight. Guido Bentivoglio was Papal Legate to the Low Countries, and wrote a history of the wars there.

Alvise Cornaro (1475-1566), an aristocratic man of letters, spent his life in Padua, the centre of university studies, where he protected scientists and scholars, and wrote a number of treatises (including *Della vita sobria*, On the sober life). Rather than emphasise his sitter's versatility, Tintoretto concentrates on his very human aspect, through a sombre harmony of greys and blacks. The portrait was acquired by Cardinal Leopoldo de' Medici.

APOLLO ROOM (SALA DI APOLLO)

The decoration was begun by Pietro da Cortona in 1646, and completed by his pupil Ciro Ferri (1659-61), following the master's design.

TITIAN

The Magdalen

c. 1555
Oil on panel, 84 × 69 cm

Signed "TITIANUS", this picture, copied by the artist himself and by his workshop in numerous versions, was painted for the court of Urbino in about 1555. The voluptuous physical beauty of the model is barely concealed by the rippling mass of auburn hair, of the colour indeed that we call "Titian". The work is characterized by the masterly harmony of chromatic tones and a technique in which painterly freedom outweighs concerns of draughtsmanship.

Titian

Portrait of a man
("The grey-eyed
nobleman" or
"Englishman")
c. 1555
Oil on canvas, 111 × 96 cm

Romantic critics have
identified the salient features of this portrait of a
young man: the atten-
tive, almost magnetic
gaze of the pale grey
eyes, and the *sprezzatu-*
ra or courtly noncha-

lance which earned it
the titles noted above
(and also the title *The*
Duke of Norfolk). In
point of fact we know
nothing about the iden-
tity of the sitter, who
must however have
been of exalted station,
as appears from the
sober but elaborate
dark suit, the heavy gold
chain, the gloves held in
the right hand, and the
faintly haughty expres-
sion. The very dimen-

sions of the portrait
must be indicative of the
patron's importance, as
too must its pictorial
quality. Here Titian has
given us one of the mas-
terpieces of his early
maturity, a subtly intro-
spective analysis of the
sitter's personality, but
also a colouristic har-
mony of tones depend-
ing on the interplay of
greys and blacks to em-
phasise the authority in
the youthful visage.

ANDREA DEL SARTO

Lamentation over the dead Christ ("Pietà di Luco")

1523-24
Oil on panel, 238 × 198 cm

This is the third Pietà (the other two being those of Perugino and of Fra' Bartolomeo) in the Pitti Gallery. Andrea del Sarto invests it with a formal monumentality derived from Michelangelo and Raphael. The colour harmonies of bright and transparent hues, with bold juxtapositions, foreshadow the achievements of the Mannerist painters, Pontormo and Rosso Fiorentino (both represented by remarkable works in the Gallery). The painting was intended for the high altar in the church of San Pietro a Luco, in the Mugello, where it was replaced by a copy (it came to the Pitti Palace in 1782).

ANDREA DEL SARTO
Madonna and Child with St Elizabeth and St John the Baptist ("Sacra Famiglia Medici")
1529
Oil on panel, 140 × 104 cm

This *Holy Family*, painted for Ottaviano de' Medici in 1529, is one of Andrea del Sarto's most important private devotional works. The composition pays tribute to the three most significant artists of the High Renaissance; Leonardo, Michelangelo and Raphael. The *sfumato* or shading effects are derived from the first, the clarity of the design and the sculptural quality of the figures from the second, and the felicitous composition from the third, clearly derived from the *Holy Families* of Raphael's Florentine period. The combination of these influences, fused with Andrea del Sarto's particular solemnity results in an individual and most appealing style.

GUIDO RENI
Cleopatra
c. 1638-39
Oil on canvas, 122 × 96 cm

The pathetic pose derived from sculpture and the accentuated lighting on the silken brushwork are typical of the style of Guido Reni. He was one of the leading figures in European painting in the middle of the seventeenth century and it was works like this which gained him the epithet "divine". The picture was commissioned by Cardinal Leopoldo de' Medici.

CARLO MARATTA
The Madonna appearing to St Philip Neri
c. 1675
Oil on canvas, 343 × 197 cm

A masterpiece by the leading painter of the Roman school at the end of the seventeenth century this painting combines the achievements of the Roman Baroque with the stylistic innovations of Guido Reni. The diagonal emphasis of the composition and the pale colouring are clearly indebted to the *Vision of Andrea Corsini*, painted for the

Barberini. This large altarpiece adorned the church of San Giovanni dei Fiorentini in Rome, before the Medici acquired it at the end of the seventeenth century.

71

VENUS ROOM (SALA DI VENERE)

The fresco and plasterwork decoration of the ceiling was executed by Pietro da Cortona from 1641-42. The centre of the ceiling shows the young prince, Cosimo III, being dragged from the arms of Venus by Pallas Athene, the goddess of War, towards Hercules, or glory. The lunettes contain episodes from antiquity alluding to the power and magnanimity of the Medici princes, while the oval stucco frames contain portraits of the Medici popes and Grand Dukes.

ANTONIO CANOVA
Venus ("Venere Italica")
1810-11
Carrara marble,
height 172 cm

This work by the greatest Neoclassical sculptor in Europe, active in the last years of the eighteenth century and the first two decades of the nineteenth, reflects Canova's "modern" interpretation of the classical *Venere callipigia*. The smooth surface finish of the marble body and the folds of the drapery reflect a supreme technical ability unparalleled since the work of Bernini some two hundred years earlier. Canova's *Venus* was commissioned as a replacement for the *Venus dei Medici* which Napoleon had taken as booty to Paris but which was returned in 1816 and now stands in the Tribuna of the Uffizi Gallery in Florence.

PETER PAUL RUBENS

Peasants returning from the fields

c. 1640
Oil on panel, 121 × 194 cm

This painting and the companion work showing *Ulysses on the island of the Phaeacians*, in the same room, are examples of landscape painting by the greatest of the Dutch Baroque painters. Rubens, who painted various views of the countryside around Malines, here creates a serene vision of the natural world with the peasants, animals and trees bathed in the warm glow of the setting sun. Both paintings originally belonged to the Duke of Richelieu and were then acquired by the Hapsburgs before being brought to Florence from Vienna by Peter Leopold of Lorraine who became Grand Duke in 1756.

SALVATOR ROSA
Harbour at sunset
c. 1645
Oil on canvas, 234 × 395 cm

This large canvas by the Neapolitan Salvator Rosa, together with the companion work depicting a *Harbour with a lighthouse*, was painted for Cardinal Giovan Carlo de' Medici during the artist's Florentine period, lasting almost ten years from 1640-49. In this grandiose yet serene view a sense of depth is created by the soft light of the setting sun, inspired by the work of Claude Lorraine. Rosa's landscapes, and there are several fine examples in the Gallery (Psyche Room), had a considerable impact on the development of the genre in the seventeenth and eighteenth centuries.

TITIAN

The concert

1510-12
Oil on canvas,
86.5 × 123.5 cm

Cardinal Leopoldo de' Medici, an enthusiastic collector of Venetian painting, bought this picture in Venice in 1654 as a work by Giorgione. The painting is now thought to be an early work by Giorgione's greatest pupil, Titian. In both style and poetical subject matter the painting is still strongly reminiscent of Giorgione's slightly unreal world (*Fête champetre*, Louvre, Paris) in which the figures appear spiritually remote, a prelude to the later interpretations of the Romantic painters.

TITIAN

Portrait of a Young Woman ("La Bella")

c. 1536
Oil on canvas, 89 × 75.5 cm

The title of *La Bella*, describing Titian's subject, a beautiful woman with fine dark eyes commanding our attention, could hardly be disputed, although her identity is still open to debate. She is dressed in a fine blue gown embroidered in gold, with full slashed sleeves with touches of white, has a gold chain, pearl earrings and a heavy golden belt. Traditionally she is identified with Francesco Maria della Rovere, the Duke of Urbino's lover. In a letter sent by the Duke to Titian in 1536 he urges the painter to send him the work, referring to the subject as the "woman in the blue dress". She was probably Titian's model for the *Venus of Urbino* (Uffizi Gallery, Florence), also commissioned by the Duke. Whatever her identity, both paintings are masterpieces of Titian's early maturity and confirm his reputation as a superb portraitist and the leading painter of the Venetian school.

TITIAN

Portrait of Pietro Aretino

c. 1545
Oil on canvas, 96.7 × 76.6 cm

This portrait marks the friendship between Titian and Aretino, the celebrated man of letters and satirist, who launched attacks on the European political scene from his base in Venice, a friendship which failed to survive the painting's comple-

tion. Aretino disliked it and accused Titian of working in haste, having little understanding of Titian's painterly technique, which became increasingly impressionistic in his later years. The writer therefore sent it to the first Grand Duke, Cosimo I, asking for a substantial payment in return. Aretino's inability to appreciate this powerful portrait, with its debt to Michelangelo in

the proud expression and bearing of the head, led to Florence acquiring one of the finest of Titian's portraits.

Royal Apartments

The Royal Apartments occupy the rooms on the west side of the Pitti Palace façade together with four more overlooking the Boboli gardens. In the second half of the seventeenth century these were the rooms reserved for the Medici Grand Prince Ferdinando (1663-1713): the eldest son of Cosimo III who never ruled as he died before his father. He decorated his apartments with an impressive collection of some thousand paintings later forming the nucleus of works displayed in the Palatine Gallery as well as enriching the Uffizi galleries. The apartments were further enlarged and completely re-decorated and refurnished, most notably after the Restoration (1814) to suit the taste of the successors to the Medici, the Grand Dukes of the House of Lorraine. In 1853 the walls of the first five rooms were given their present sumptuous silk wall covering and supplied with French carpets. With the accession of the Savoy the Pitti became for a brief period the official residence of the ruling family of the newly united Kingdom of Italy and the alterations to the palace date largely from the reign of Umberto I and Margherita of Savoy. In the 1880s furniture, paintings and other precious objects were brought from the Ducal palace in Parma including an important group of portraits of the French royal family at the time of Louis XV.

The entrance to the Apartments is through the Sala delle Nicchie, named after the six niches, there were originally ten, housing Roman copies of Greek sculpture, first displayed here at the end of the sixteenth century.

GREEN ROOM (SALA VERDE)

The walls are covered in a well preserved, luxurious green silk and hung with some fine eighteenth-century French paintings. The room also houses some of the oldest pieces of furniture belonging to the Medici.

JEAN MARC NATTIER
Henriette of France dressed as Flora
1742
Oil on canvas,
94.5 × 128.5 cm

This elegant work rises above the usual characteristics of the historical portrait, transforming it into a mythological representation transfused with all the charm of the rococo world. A similar portrait of Henriette of France (1727-52) exists at Versailles. She was the twin sister of Louise Elisabeth and so one of the eldest daughters of Louis XV and Maria Leczinska (their portraits are in the same room).

CARAVAGGIO

Portrait of Fra'
Marcantonio
Martelli
c. 1609
Oil on canvas, 115 × 95 cm

Documents have recently made it possible to identify the Knight of Malta depicted here. Martelli, belonged to a noble Florentine family and sat for this impressive portrait in about 1609 when Caravaggio was in Sicily. The attribution of the painting, mentioned with no reference to its author in a seventeenth century inventory of the Palace, to Caravaggio is now unanimously accepted.

THRONE ROOM (SALA DEL TRONO)

This room, covered in red brocade, was the chamberlain's room during the Lorraine period before gaining its present appearance under the Savoy. The ceiling decoration is by Giuseppe Castagnoli.

BLUE ROOM (SALA CELESTE)

Covered in very worn blue silk made in the early nineteenth century, only some of the "mantovane" drapes covering the windows and doors have survived. The walls are hung with wonderful portraits of the Medici by Justus Susstermans.

Chapel (Cappella)

Once the alcove of Grand Prince Ferdinando de' Medici the decorative stucco and carving of that period still survive. It was transformed into a chapel in the first half of the eighteenth century and houses some intriguing paintings including the Madonna delle Rose *by Botticelli and assistants.*

ANTHONIE VAN DYCK
Portrait of a noblewoman
1623
Oil on paper, 34×27 cm, applied to canvas, 55×43 cm

A sketch on paper for one of van Dyck's portraits from his Genoese period (1621-27) of Caterina Durazzo Adorno and children, known as *The Golden lady* (Galleria Durazzo Pallavicini, Genoa), this work has all the freshness and brilliance of brushwork to be expected from Van Dyck.

ROOM OF THE PARROTS (SALA DEI PAPPAGALLI)

The room takes its name from the birds on the beautiful Neo-Classical silk wall-covering which are not parrots but Imperial eagles.

LUCAS CRANACH
Portrait of a young woman
c. 1520-30
Oil on canvas, 38 × 26.5 cm

DOMENICO PULIGO
The Magdalen
c. 1515
Oil on canvas, 61 × 51 cm

This small portrait is typical of the Cranach's workshop production which, in the 1530s, produced a series of portraits of elegantly dressed young women, as commissions of this kind were in wide demand. This portrait, most memorable for the young lady's fine ruby-red gown embroidered in gold, is very similar to to one in the National Gallery in London. There can be no certainly about the painting's provenance but it was possibly one of many brought to Florence from Vienna by the Lorraines.

Domenico Puligo was an enthusiastic exponent of Leonardo's *sfumato* technique which had an immediate impact on Florentine painting in the early years of the sixteenth century. His paintings, also reminiscent of the style of Andrea del Sarto, appear as rather flat and impersonal interpretations of many of his contemporaries' innovations from Leonardo to Fra' Bartolomeo. This Magdalen, one of several versions, is one of his more successful paintings.

Queen's Apartment (Appartamento della Regina)

The rooms of the Queen's Apartment are; the yellow drawing room (left), her bedroom (below), the oval and round drawing rooms are all lined with silk, and decorated with furniture, paintings and porcelain reflecting the taste of two hundred years, from the seventeenth to the nineteenth centuries.

KING'S APARTMENT (APPARTAMENTO DEL RE)

The King's Apartment cinsisting of four rooms: a bedroom (left), a study in-cluding French and Tuscan furniture and ornaments of the eighteenth and nineteenth centuries, the red drawing room (below), also with French and Tuscan furniture and a collection of Romantic paintings, followed by the an-techamber with a Landscape *painted in 1868 by Antonio Fontanesi and* The rape of Piccarda Donati *painted between 1865-70 by Raffaello Sorbi.*

INDEX OF ARTISTS AND WORKS

Pietro da Cortona, The golden age,
detail of the decoration of the Stove Room.

printed in October 2002
by Media Print-Livorno
for
s i l l a b e

www.sillabe.it
info@sillabe.it